contents

NZ, Canada, US and UK readers
Please note that Australian cup and
spoon measurements are metric.
A conversion chart appears on page 62.

prawn and green onion skewers

1.5kg uncooked medium prawns
2 tablespoons lime juice
1 tablespoon olive oil
2 cloves garlic, crushed
12 green onions

1 Shell and devein prawns, leaving tails intact. Combine prawns in medium bowl with juice, oil and garlic. Cover; refrigerate 1 hour.
2 Cut onions into 4cm lengths. Thread prawns and onion alternately onto skewers. Cook on heated oiled grill plate (or grill or barbecue) until prawns change colour.

serves 4
preparation time 25 minutes (plus refrigeration time)
cooking time 10 minutes
per serving 6g fat; 920kJ (220 cal)
tip Soak 12 bamboo skewers in water for at least 1 hour prior to use, to prevent them from scorching and splintering during cooking. If using metal skewers, oil them first to stop the prawns from sticking.

salt and pepper prawns

Prawns can be peeled and skewered up to 6 hours ahead. Barbecue just before serving.

1kg uncooked large prawns
2 teaspoons sea salt
¼ teaspoon five-spice powder
½ teaspoon cracked
   black pepper

1 Peel and devein prawns, leaving tails intact. Thread one prawn onto each skewer lengthways.
2 Combine remaining ingredients in small bowl.
3 Cook prawns on heated oiled grill plate (or grill or barbecue), uncovered, until browned all over and changed in colour; sprinkle with half the salt mixture during cooking.
4 Serve prawns with remaining salt mixture.

serves 4
preparation time 20 minutes
cooking time 10 minutes
per serving 0.8g fat; 467kJ (111 cal)
tip If using bamboo skewers, soak them in water for at least 1 hour before using, to avoid scorching and splintering during cooking.

prawn kebabs with chilli lime sauce

1kg uncooked medium prawns
2 cloves garlic, crushed
1 tablespoon finely chopped
    fresh lemon grass
1 tablespoon balsamic vinegar
1 tablespoon coarsely chopped
    fresh coriander
1 tablespoon peanut oil
4 green onions
chilli lime sauce
⅔ cup (150g) white sugar
½ cup (125ml) water
1 teaspoon finely
    grated lime rind
2 fresh small red thai chillies,
    chopped finely
2 tablespoons sweet chilli sauce
⅓ cup (80ml) lime juice

1   Make chilli lime sauce.
2   Shell and devein prawns, leaving tails intact.
3   Combine garlic, lemon grass, vinegar, coriander and oil in large bowl; add prawns. Cover; refrigerate 3 hours or overnight.
4   Drain prawns; discard marinade.
5   Cut onions into 5cm lengths. Thread onion and prawns onto eight skewers.
6   Cook prawns on heated oiled grill plate (or grill or barbecue), uncovered, until changed in colour. Serve prawns with chilli lime sauce.

chilli lime sauce Combine sugar and the water in small saucepan; stir over heat, without boiling, until sugar dissolves. Simmer, uncovered, without stirring, 5 minutes. Add rind, chilli and sauce; simmer, uncovered, 5 minutes. Stir in juice; cool.

serves 4
preparation time 40 minutes
(plus refrigeration time)
cooking time 25 minutes
per serving 5.7g fat; 1321kJ (315 cal)
tips Soak bamboo skewers in water for at least 1 hour before using, to avoid scorching and splintering during cooking. If using metal skewers, oil them first to stop the prawns from sticking.

pesto fish kebabs

600g firm white fish fillets
1 tablespoon bottled basil pesto
½ cup finely chopped fresh flat-leaf parsley
½ small cabbage (600g), shredded finely
⅓ cup (65g) rinsed, drained baby capers
1 teaspoon finely grated lemon rind
½ cup finely chopped fresh mint

1 Cut fish into 2cm cubes; combine with pesto and 1 tablespoon of the parsley in medium bowl. Cover; refrigerate 1 hour.
2 Thread fish onto eight skewers.
3 Cook fish on heated oiled grill plate (or grill or barbecue), uncovered, until browned and just cooked through. Cover to keep warm.
4 Cook cabbage on heated oiled barbecue plate, uncovered, until just tender. Stir in capers, rind, mint and remaining parsley.
5 Serve fish with cabbage mixture.

serves 4
preparation time 20 minutes (plus refrigeration time)
cooking time 15 minutes
per serving 5.5g fat; 870kJ (208 cal)
tip Soak bamboo skewers in water for at least 1 hour before using, to avoid scorching and splintering during cooking.

cajun seafood kebabs with avocado salsa

800g uncooked medium
 prawns
800g firm white fish fillets
2 tablespoons cajun
 seasoning
2 teaspoons ground cumin
2 tablespoons coarsely
 chopped fresh oregano
2 cloves garlic, crushed
¼ cup (60ml) olive oil
avocado salsa
1 large avocado (320g),
 chopped finely
3 medium tomatoes (570g),
 seeded, chopped finely
1 small red onion (100g),
 chopped finely
2 tablespoons finely chopped
 fresh coriander
2 tablespoons lemon juice
1 tablespoon olive oil
½ teaspoon white sugar

1 Peel and devein prawns leaving tails intact.
Cut fish into 3cm pieces.
2 Combine prawns and fish with remaining
ingredients in medium bowl. Cover; refrigerate
1 hour.
3 Thread prawns and fish onto 12 skewers.
Cook seafood on heated oiled grill plate (or grill
or barbecue), uncovered, until cooked.
4 Meanwhile, make avocado salsa.
5 Serve seafood kebabs with avocado salsa.
avocado salsa Combine ingredients in
medium bowl.

serves 6
preparation time 30 minutes
cooking time 10 minutes
per serving 24.2g fat; 1681kJ (401 cal)
tip Soak bamboo skewers in water for at least
1 hour before using, to avoid scorching and
splintering during cooking.

herbed swordfish kebabs

2kg swordfish steaks
4 medium lemons (560g)
⅓ cup finely chopped fresh coriander
½ cup finely chopped fresh flat-leaf parsley
½ cup finely chopped fresh chives
½ teaspoon freshly ground black pepper
2 tablespoons peanut oil

1 Remove and discard skin from fish; cut fish into 3cm pieces.
2 Using zester, remove as much of the rind as possible from lemons. Squeeze ⅔ cup juice from the lemons.
3 Combine fish rind, juice, herbs, pepper and oil in large bowl.
4 Thread fish onto 16 skewers; place, in single layer, in large shallow dish. Pour any remaining marinade over skewers. Cover; refrigerate 3 hours or overnight.
5 Cook skewers on heated oiled grill plate (or grill or barbecue) until browned all over and cooked through. Serve with baby spinach leaves, if you like.

serves 8
preparation time 30 minutes (plus refrigeration time)
cooking time 15 minutes
per serving 11.8g fat; 1346kJ (322 cal)
tip Soak bamboo skewers in water for at least 1 hour before using, to avoid scorching and splintering during cooking.

lamb kebabs with baba ghanoush

Baba ghanoush is a Middle Eastern-style eggplant dip, available at supermarkets and delicatessens.

1kg minced lamb
¼ cup coarsely chopped fresh flat-leaf parsley
2 tablespoons coarsely chopped fresh coriander
1 egg yolk
2 teaspoons ground cumin
1 teaspoon garam masala
½ teaspoon ground cinnamon
2 cloves garlic, crushed
200g prepared baba ghanoush

1 Combine lamb, parsley, coriander, egg yolk, spices and garlic in large bowl.
2 Roll tablespoons of mixture into oval shapes; shape two pieces of lamb mixture onto each skewer.
3 Cook kebabs on heated oiled grill plate (or grill or barbecue) until browned all over and cooked as desired.
4 Serve kebabs with baba ghanoush.

serves 6
preparation time 30 minutes
cooking time 10 minutes
per serving 24g fat; 1571kJ (375 cal)
tip Soak bamboo skewers in water for at least 1 hour before using, to avoid scorching and splintering during cooking.

lamb souvlakia

1.5kg boned lamb shoulder
¼ cup (60ml) olive oil
2 teaspoons finely grated
    lemon rind
½ cup (125ml) lemon juice
2 cloves garlic, crushed
2 tablespoons finely chopped
    fresh oregano
1½ cups (420g) plain yogurt
2 lebanese cucumbers (260g),
    seeded, chopped finely
2 cloves garlic, crushed, extra
8 large pitta
4 medium tomatoes (760g),
    sliced thinly

1 Trim fat from lamb; cut lamb into 3cm pieces.
Combine oil, rind, juice, garlic and oregano in
large bowl; add lamb. Cover; refrigerate 3 hours
or overnight.
2 Meanwhile, combine yogurt, cucumber and
extra garlic in small bowl. Cover; refrigerate
3 hours or overnight.
3 Thread lamb onto 16 skewers. Cook lamb
on heated oiled grill plate (or grill or barbecue),
uncovered, until browned and cooked through.
4 Serve souvlakia with cucumber yogurt, pitta
and tomato.

serves 8
preparation time 40 minutes
(plus refrigeration time)
cooking time 15 minutes
per serving 21.5g fat; 2678kJ (640 cal)
tip Soak bamboo skewers in water for at least
1 hour before using, to avoid scorching and
splintering during cooking.

lamb kofta with hummus and tabouleh

½ cup (80g) burghul
1kg minced lamb
1 small brown onion (80g),
    chopped finely
1 teaspoon allspice
1 clove garlic, crushed
1 cup (75g) stale breadcrumbs
1 egg, beaten lightly
¾ cup (210g) plain yogurt
¼ cup finely chopped
    fresh mint

hummus

2 x 300g cans chickpeas,
    rinsed, drained
1 teaspoon salt
1 clove garlic, quartered
⅓ cup (80ml) tahini
¼ cup (60ml) lemon juice
⅓ cup (80ml) water

tabouleh

¼ cup (40g) burghul
2 medium tomatoes (380g),
    seeded, chopped finely
4 cups coarsely chopped
    fresh flat-leaf parsley
1 small red onion (100g),
    chopped finely
2 tablespoons lemon juice
2 tablespoons olive oil

1 Cover burghul with cold water in small bowl; stand 20 minutes or until burghul softens. Drain burghul, squeezing with hands to remove as much water as possible.
2 Meanwhile, make tabouleh.
3 Combine burghul with lamb, onion, allspice, garlic, breadcrumbs and egg in large bowl. Divide mixture into 12 balls; mould balls around 12 skewers to form sausage shape.
4 Cook kofta on heated oiled grill plate (or grill or barbecue), uncovered, until browned and cooked through.
5 Meanwhile, make hummus.
6 Serve kofta with hummus, tabouleh and combined yogurt and mint.
tabouleh Cover burghul with cold water in small bowl; stand 10 minutes or until burghul softens. Drain burghul, squeezing with hands to remove as much water as possible. Combine burghul in large bowl with remaining ingredients.
hummus Blend or process ingredients until almost smooth.

serves 6
preparation time 1 hour (plus standing time)
cooking time 15 minutes
per serving 35g fat; 2731kJ (653 cal)
tips Soak bamboo skewers in water for at least 1 hour before using, to avoid scorching and splintering during cooking.
Lamb can be replaced with minced beef or chicken, if preferred.

lamb and haloumi kebabs

750g diced lamb
200g semi-dried tomatoes
400g haloumi cheese, chopped coarsely
⅓ cup (80ml) red wine vinegar
2 cloves garlic, crushed
⅓ cup (80ml) olive oil

1 Thread lamb, tomato and cheese onto eight skewers.
2 Place kebabs in shallow dish; pour over combined remaining ingredients. Cover; refrigerate 3 hours or overnight.
3 Drain kebabs; discard marinade. Cook kebabs on heated oiled grill plate (or grill or barbecue), until cooked as desired.

serves 4
preparation time 30 minutes (plus refrigeration time)
cooking time 15 minutes
per serving 42.9g fat; 3048kJ (728 cal)
tip Soak bamboo skewers in water for at least 1 hour before using, to avoid scorching and splintering during cooking.

beef skewers on lettuce cups

500g beef rump steak,
  sliced thinly
½ telegraph cucumber (200g),
  peeled, halved then
    quartered lengthways
6 green onions, cut into 5cm
  lengths, then into thin strips
1 cup (80g) bean sprouts
1 large carrot (180g), cut into
  5cm lengths, then into strips
8 lettuce leaves
marinade
2 tablespoons finely chopped
  fresh lemon grass
1 medium white onion (150g),
  sliced thinly
2 cloves garlic, crushed
2 teaspoons white sugar
2 fresh small red thai chillies,
  chopped finely
2 teaspoons sesame oil
2 teaspoons sesame seeds
garlic chilli sauce
2 cloves garlic, chopped finely
1 fresh small red thai chilli,
  chopped finely
1 tablespoon white sugar
2 tablespoons lime juice
¼ cup (60ml) rice vinegar
¼ cup (60ml) fish sauce
¼ cup (60ml) water

1 Make marinade.
2 Combine beef and marinade in large bowl.
Cover; refrigerate 3 hours or overnight.
3 Thread beef onto 16 skewers. Cook beef
on heated oiled grill plate (or grill or barbecue),
uncovered, until cooked as desired.
4 Meanwhile, make garlic chilli sauce.
5 Divide cucumber, onion, sprouts and carrot
among lettuce leaves. Top with beef; drizzle
with sauce.
marinade Combine ingredients in small bowl.
garlic chilli sauce Blend or process ingredients
until combined.

serves 4
preparation time 45 minutes
(plus refrigeration time)
cooking time 10 minutes
per serving 9.2g fat; 1118kJ (267 cal)
tip Soak bamboo skewers in water for at least
1 hour before using, to avoid scorching and
splintering during cooking.

beef and onion kebabs

700g beef rump steak
18 baby onions (450g), halved
marinade
½ cup (125ml) tomato sauce
½ cup (175g) honey
½ cup (125ml) lemon juice
2 tablespoons finely chopped fresh oregano
4cm piece fresh ginger (20g), grated
1 tablespoon worcestershire sauce

1 Make marinade.
2 Cut beef into 3cm pieces.
3 Thread beef and onion, alternately, onto 12 skewers. Place kebabs
in shallow dish; add marinade. Cover; refrigerate 3 hours or overnight.
4 Cook kebabs on heated oiled grill plate (or grill or barbecue), uncovered,
until browned and cooked as desired.
marinade Combine ingredients in medium jug.

serves 4
preparation time 20 minutes (plus refrigeration time)
cooking time 10 minutes
per serving 8.3g fat; 1872kJ (447 cal)
tip Soak bamboo skewers in water for at least 1 hour before using,
to avoid scorching and splintering during cooking.

teriyaki beef kebabs

800g beef rump steak, chopped coarsely
2 medium brown onions (300g), chopped coarsely
marinade
1 cup (250ml) teriyaki marinade
2 cloves garlic, crushed
4cm piece fresh ginger (20g), grated
1 tablespoon peanut oil
2 teaspoons lemon juice

1 Make marinade.
2 Combine beef and marinade in large bowl. Cover; refrigerate
3 hours or overnight.
3 Thread beef and onion, alternately, onto eight bamboo skewers.
Cook kebabs on heated oiled grill plate (or grill or barbecue), uncovered,
until browned and cooked as desired.
marinade Combine ingredients in medium bowl.

serves 4
preparation time 20 minutes (plus refrigeration time)
cooking time 15 minutes
per serving 13.9g fat; 1624kJ (388 cal)
tip Soak bamboo skewers in water for at least 1 hour before using,
to avoid scorching and splintering during cooking.

spiced pork skewers with honey glaze

500g pork fillets
2 cloves garlic, crushed
2 teaspoons cumin seeds
½ teaspoon ground coriander
¼ teaspoon sweet paprika
1 tablespoon olive oil
honey glaze
½ cup (125ml) orange juice
2 tablespoons honey
2 tablespoons barbecue
  sauce
1 teaspoon dijon mustard

1   Make honey glaze.
2   Cut pork into 3cm cubes. Combine pork with garlic, cumin, coriander, paprika and oil in medium bowl.
3   Thread pork onto eight skewers. Cook pork on heated oiled grill plate (or grill or barbecue), uncovered, until browned and cooked through. Serve with honey glaze.
honey glaze   Combine ingredients in small saucepan; stir over heat until boiling. Reduce heat; simmer about 5 minutes or until thickened.

makes 8
preparation time 15 minutes
cooking time 15 minutes
per skewer 2.6g fat; 357kJ (85 cal)
tip Soak bamboo skewers in water for at least 1 hour before using, to avoid scorching and splintering during cooking.

hoisin pork kebabs

½ cup (125ml) hoisin sauce
2 tablespoons plum sauce
2 cloves garlic, crushed
750g pork fillet, sliced thinly
2 green onions
1 lebanese cucumber (130g)

1 Combine pork, sauces and garlic in large bowl. Cover; refrigerate 3 hours or overnight.
2 Thread pork onto 12 skewers. Cook pork on heated oiled grill plate (or grill or barbecue), uncovered, until browned and cooked through.
3 Meanwhile, thinly slice onions diagonally. Halve cucumber lengthways; discard seeds. Thinly slice cucumber lengthways.
4 Serve pork with onion, cucumber and extra plum sauce, if you like.

serves 4
preparation time 35 minutes (plus refrigeration time)
cooking time 15 minutes
per serving 6.3g fat; 1273kJ (304 cal)
tip Soak bamboo skewers in water for at least 1 hour before using, to avoid scorching and splintering during cooking.

chicken, lemon and artichoke skewers

3 medium lemons (420g)
2 cloves garlic, crushed
¼ cup (60ml) olive oil
600g chicken breast fillets, chopped coarsely
800g canned artichoke hearts, drained, halved
24 button mushrooms

1 Squeeze juice from one lemon (you will need two tablespoons of juice). Combine juice, garlic and oil in small screw-top jar; shake well.
2 Cut remaining lemons into 24 wedges. Thread chicken, artichoke, mushrooms and lemon, alternately, onto 12 skewers.
3 Cook skewers on heated oiled grill plate (or grill or barbecue) until cooked through. Brush with oil mixture during cooking.

serves 4
preparation time 20 minutes
cooking time 10 minutes
per serving 22.6g fat; 1534kJ (367 cal)
tip Soak bamboo skewers in water for at least 1 hour before using, to avoid scorching and splintering during cooking.

lime chicken on lemon grass skewers

6 long fresh lemon grass stalks
⅓ cup (80ml) peanut oil
1 tablespoon grated lime rind
¼ cup finely chopped fresh coriander
6 chicken breast fillets (1kg)
¼ cup (60ml) lime juice
2 fresh small red thai chillies, chopped finely
⅓ cup (80ml) macadamia oil
1 tablespoon raw sugar
1 clove garlic, crushed

1 Cut 3cm off the bottom end of each lemon grass stalk; reserve stalks. Chop the 3cm pieces finely; combine in large shallow dish with peanut oil, rind and coriander.
2 Cut each fillet into three strips crossways. thread three strips onto each lemon grass skewer. Place skewers in dish with lemon grass marinade; turn skewers to coat chicken in marinade. Cover; refrigerate 3 hours or overnight.
3 Cook skewers on heated oiled grill plate (or grill or barbecue), uncovered, until chicken is cooked through.
4 Meanwhile, combine remaining ingredients in screw-top jar; shake well. Serve with chicken skewers.

serves 6
preparation time 20 minutes (plus refrigeration time)
cooking time 15 minutes
per serving 33.6g fat; 1907kJ (456 cal)
tip To make it easier to thread the chicken onto the lemon grass skewers, use a thick bamboo skewer to pierce the chicken pieces first.

mint and ginger chicken skewers

700g chicken breast fillets
8 long fresh lemon grass stalks
¼ cup (60ml) peanut oil
2 cloves garlic, crushed
4cm piece fresh ginger (20g),
    grated
2 tablespoons coarsely
    chopped fresh mint
2 tablespoons coarsely
    chopped fresh basil

1 Cut chicken into 3cm pieces; thread chicken onto lemon grass skewers.

2 Place skewers in shallow dish; pour over combined remaining ingredients. Cover; refrigerate 3 hours or overnight.

3 Drain chicken; discard marinade. Cook chicken on heated oiled grill plate (or grill or barbecue), uncovered, until browned and cooked through.

serves 4
preparation time 25 minutes
plus refrigeration time)
cooking time 15 minutes
per serving 23.4g fat; 1511kJ (361 cal)
tip To make it easier to thread the chicken onto the lemon grass skewers, use a thick bamboo skewer to pierce the chicken pieces first.

glazed chicken sticks

1kg chicken wings
4 green onions, chopped finely
½ cup (125ml) green ginger wine
¼ cup (60ml) light soy sauce
¼ cup (60ml) dark soy sauce
1 tablespoon brown sugar

1 Cut chicken wings into three pieces at joints; discard tips. Holding small end of bone, trim around bone with sharp knife to cut meat free from bone. Cut, scrape and push meat down to large end (half of the pieces will have an extra fine bone that should be removed).
2 Using fingers, pull skin and meat down over end of bone; each piece will resemble a baby drumstick.
3 Combine onion, wine, sauces and sugar in large bowl; add chicken. Cover; refrigerate 3 hours or overnight.
4 Drain chicken; discard marinade. Cook chicken on heated oiled grill plate (or grill or barbecue), uncovered, until browned and cooked through.

serves 6
preparation time 35 minutes (plus refrigeration time)
cooking time 10 minutes
per serving 16g fat; 1078kJ (258 cal)

chicken kebabs with coriander pesto

2 teaspoons finely grated
  lime rind
2 tablespoons lime juice
1 teaspoon ground coriander
1 tablespoon peanut oil
700g chicken breast fillets,
  chopped coarsely
¼ cup (35g) unsalted peanuts,
  roasted, chopped coarsely
coriander pesto
2 tablespoons unsalted
  peanuts, roasted
½ cup firmly packed fresh
  coriander leaves
2 cloves garlic, crushed
½ cup (125ml) peanut oil

1 Combine rind, juice, coriander and oil in large bowl; add chicken. Cover; refrigerate 3 hours or overnight.

2 Drain chicken; discard marinade. Thread chicken onto 12 skewers. Cook chicken on heated oiled grill plate (or grill or barbecue), uncovered, until cooked through.

4 Meanwhile, make coriander pesto.

5 Serve chicken with coriander pesto; sprinkle with nuts.

coriander pesto Blend or process ingredients until combined.

serves 6
preparation time 35 minutes
(plus refrigeration time)
cooking time 10 minutes
per serving 33g fat; 1713kJ (409 cal)
tip Soak bamboo skewers in water for at least 1 hour before using, to avoid scorching and splintering during cooking.

chicken satay

12 chicken thigh fillets (1.3kg)
2 tablespoons sweet chilli sauce
1 tablespoon peanut oil
1 clove garlic, crushed
2 tablespoons coarsely chopped fresh coriander
peanut sauce
1 cup (250ml) chicken stock
½ cup (130g) crunchy peanut butter
¼ cup (60ml) sweet chilli sauce
1 tablespoon lemon juice

1 Cut each chicken fillet into four strips lengthways.
2 Combine sauce, oil, garlic and coriander in medium bowl; add chicken.
Cover; refrigerate 3 hours or overnight.
3 Thread chicken onto 12 skewers. Cook chicken on heated oiled grill
plate (or grill or barbecue), uncovered, until browned and cooked through.
4 Meanwhile, make peanut sauce.
5 Serve chicken with peanut sauce and, if desired, rice and bok choy.
peanut sauce Combine ingredients in medium saucepan; simmer, stirring,
about 3 minutes or until sauce thickens slightly.

serves 6
preparation time 30 minutes (plus refrigeration time)
cooking time 15 minutes
per serving 30.2g fat; 2011kJ (481 cal)
tips Soak bamboo skewers in water for at least 1 hour before using,
to avoid scorching and splintering during cooking.
Uncooked marinated skewers are suitable to freeze; the peanut sauce
is suitable to microwave.

herbed chicken kebabs
with roasted pecans

1kg chicken breast fillets, sliced thinly
½ cup finely chopped fresh chives
⅓ cup finely chopped fresh oregano
¼ cup finely chopped fresh marjoram
4 cloves garlic, crushed
1 tablespoon lemon pepper seasoning
2 tablespoons chicken stock
¼ cup (30g) coarsely chopped pecans, roasted

1   Thread chicken onto 12 skewers.
2   Combine chives, oregano, marjoram, garlic, seasoning and stock in
shallow dish; add chicken. Cover; refrigerate 3 hours or overnight.
3   Cook chicken on heated oiled grill plate (or grill or barbecue), uncovered,
until cooked through.
4   Serve kebabs with pecans, and a green leafy salad, if desired.

serves 6
preparation time 15 minutes (plus refrigeration time)
cooking time 15 minutes
per serving 12.9g fat; 1118kJ (267 cal)
tip Soak bamboo skewers in water for at least 1 hour before using,
to avoid scorching and splintering during cooking.

bombay-spiced chicken skewers

⅓ cup (80ml) peanut oil
4 cloves garlic, crushed
2 tablespoons sweet paprika
1 tablespoon ground cumin
1 tablespoon ground turmeric
1 tablespoon ground coriander
2kg chicken breast fillets
raita
2 lebanese cucumbers (260g), seeded, chopped finely
¾ cup (210g) plain yogurt
1 tablespoon lemon juice
2 cloves garlic, crushed
¼ cup finely chopped fresh mint

1 Heat oil in medium frying pan; cook garlic and spices, stirring, until fragrant; cool.
2 Cut chicken into 3cm pieces. Thread onto 24 skewers; place chicken in large shallow dish. Pour over spiced oil mixture; turn chicken to coat well. Cover; refrigerate 3 hours or overnight.
3 Drain chicken; discard marinade. Cook chicken on heated oiled grill plate (or grill or barbecue), uncovered, until browned and cooked through.
4 Meanwhile, make raita. Serve chicken with raita.
raita Combine ingredients in small bowl.

serves 8
preparation time 30 minutes (plus refrigeration time)
cooking time 15 minutes
per serving 29.5 fat; 2096kJ (501 cal)
tip Soak bamboo skewers in water for at least 1 hour before using, to avoid scorching and splintering during cooking.

yakitori chicken

Yakitori is a popular Japanese snack – skewers of grilled chicken pieces, served with a dipping sauce, are consumed with sake after a hard day at the office by thousands of executives.

1kg chicken breast fillets
¼ cup (60ml) mirin
½ cup (125ml) light soy sauce
2cm piece fresh ginger (10g), grated
2 cloves garlic, crushed
¼ teaspoon freshly ground black pepper
1 tablespoon white sugar

1 Cut chicken into 2cm pieces. Combine chicken with remaining ingredients in large bowl. Drain chicken over small bowl; reserve marinade.
2 Thread chicken onto 12 bamboo skewers. Cook skewers on heated oiled grill plate (or grill or barbecue), turning and brushing occasionally with reserved marinade, until chicken is cooked through.

serves 4
preparation time 15 minutes
cooking time 10 minutes
per serving 13.8g fat; 1614kJ (386 cal)
tips Soak bamboo skewers in water for at least 1 hour before using, to avoid scorching and splintering during cooking.
Mirin is a somewhat sweet rice wine used in many Asian, especially Japanese, dishes. You can substitute sherry or sweet white wine for mirin, if you prefer.

vegetable kebabs with balsamic dressing

250g cherry tomatoes
1 large green capsicum (350g), chopped coarsely
6 small flat mushrooms (600g), quartered
6 yellow patty-pan squash (240g), halved
3 baby eggplant (180g), sliced thickly
3 small zucchini (270g), sliced thickly
1 medium brown onion (150g), sliced thickly
500g haloumi cheese, cubed
60g baby rocket leaves
balsamic dressing
⅓ cup (80ml) olive oil
¼ cup (60ml) balsamic vinegar
1 teaspoon white sugar

1 Thread vegetables and cheese onto 12 skewers.
2 Cook kebabs, in batches, on heated oiled grill plate (or grill or barbecue) until browned all over.
3 Meanwhile, make balsamic dressing.
4 Serve kebabs on rocket leaves drizzled with balsamic dressing.
balsamic dressing Combine ingredients in screw-top jar; shake well.

serves 4
preparation time 20 minutes
cooking time 20 minutes
per serving 40.8g fat; 2402kJ (575 cal)
tip Soak bamboo skewers in water for at least 1 hour before using, to avoid scorching and splintering during cooking.

vegetarian skewers

Bocconcini, which translates from Italian as "little mouthfuls", are delectably creamy balls of fresh mozzarella. It is available in two sizes, one about as big as a walnut and the other (which we used here) even smaller, commonly referred to as cherry bocconcini.

2 tablespoons sun-dried tomato pesto
¼ cup (60ml) lemon juice
2 tablespoons olive oil
1 small red onion (100g), quartered
1 small green capsicum (150g), chopped coarsely
6 vegetarian sausages (300g), sliced thickly
250g cherry tomatoes, halved
100g ciabatta, diced into 2cm pieces
8 cherry bocconcini (80g)

1 Combine pesto, juice and oil in small bowl.
2 Thread onion, capsicum, sausage and half the tomato, alternately, onto eight skewers. Thread bread, cheese and remaining tomato, alternately, onto four skewers.
3 Brush skewers with pesto mixture; cook on heated oiled grill plate (or grill or barbecue), uncovered, brushing occasionally with pesto mixture, until skewers are browned lightly. Divide skewers among serving plates; drizzle with remaining pesto mixture.

serves 4
preparation time 10 minutes
cooking time 10 minutes
per serving 22.4g fat; 1515kJ (362 cal)
tip Soak bamboo skewers in water for at least 1 hour before using, to avoid scorching and splintering during cooking.

eggplant and haloumi skewers
with roasted tomato sauce

*You need 36 toothpicks for
this recipe.*

1 medium eggplant (300g)
250g haloumi cheese
¼ cup (35g) plain flour
1 egg, beaten lightly
½ cup (35g) fresh
   breadcrumbs
½ cup (40g) finely grated
   parmesan cheese
36 medium fresh basil leaves
vegetable oil, for deep-frying
roasted tomato sauce
125g cherry tomatoes
cooking-oil spray
1 clove garlic, crushed
½ teaspoon white sugar
1 teaspoon red wine vinegar
1 tablespoon olive oil

1 Make roasted tomato sauce.
2 Meanwhile, cut eggplant into 36 squares.
Cut haloumi into 36 squares.
3 Coat eggplant squares in flour, shake off
excess; dip into egg then coat in combined
breadcrumbs and parmesan.
4 Thread one piece of eggplant, one basil leaf
and one piece of haloumi onto each toothpick.
Heat oil in wok, deep-fry skewers, in batches,
about 30 seconds or until browned lightly;
drain on absorbent paper.
5 Serve with roasted tomato sauce.
roasted tomato sauce Preheat oven to
180°C/160°C fan-forced; line oven tray with
baking paper. Place tomatoes on tray; spray
with oil. Roast, uncovered, about 15 minutes
or until soft. Blend or process tomatoes with
remaining ingredients until smooth. Cool to
room temperature.

makes 36
preparation time 35 minutes
(plus cooling time)
cooking time 20 minutes
per toothpick 3.4g fat; 196kJ (47 cal)

fruit skewers with honey yogurt

½ medium pineapple (625g)
2 large oranges (600g)
250g strawberries
2 large bananas (460g)
30g butter
¼ cup (55g) brown sugar
1 tablespoon lemon juice
1 cup (280g) honey yogurt

1 Peel pineapple; remove and discard core. Cut pineapple into 2.5cm lengths; cut lengths crossways into 3cm pieces. Peel oranges thickly to remove bitter white pith; separate orange segments. Remove hulls from strawberries; cut in half crossways. Peel bananas; cut into 3cm slices.

2 Thread fruit, alternating varieties, onto twelve 20cm wooden skewers; place on oven tray.

3 Combine butter, sugar and juice in small saucepan over low heat, stirring until butter melts and sugar dissolves. Pour butter mixture over skewers, making sure that all fruits are coated in mixture.

4 Cook skewers, in batches, on heated lightly greased grill plate (or grill or barbecue) about 5 minutes or until browned lightly.

5 Serve skewers with yogurt.

serves 4
preparation time 30 minutes
cooking time 10 minutes
per serving 8.5g fat; 1352kJ (323 cal)
tip Soak bamboo skewers in water for at least 1 hour before using, to avoid scorching and splintering during cooking.

tropical fruit skewers with coconut dressing

2 medium bananas (400g), unpeeled
½ medium pineapple (625g), unpeeled
2 large starfruit (320g)
1 large mango (600g), chopped coarsely
coconut dressing
⅓ cup (80ml) coconut-flavoured liqueur
¼ cup (60ml) light coconut milk
1 tablespoon grated palm sugar
1cm piece fresh ginger (5g), grated

1 Make coconut dressing.
2 Cut each unpeeled banana into eight pieces. Cut unpeeled pineapple into eight slices; cut slices in half. Cut each starfruit into eight slices.
3 Thread fruit onto 8 skewers, alternating varieties. Cook skewers on grill plate (or grill or barbecue), brushing with a little of the dressing, until browned lightly. Serve skewers drizzled with remaining dressing.
coconut dressing Combine ingredients in screw-top jar; shake well.

serves 4
preparation time 30 minutes
cooking time 5 minutes
per serving 1.3g fat; 1041kJ (249 cal)
tips Soak bamboo skewers in water for at least 1 hour before using, to avoid scorching and splintering during cooking.
We used Malibu for the dressing, but you can use any coconut-flavoured liqueur you like.

glossary

allspice also known as pimento or jamaican pepper; so-named because is tastes like a combination of nutmeg, cumin, clove and cinnamon – all spices.

artichoke hearts tender centre of globe artichoke; purchased in brine canned or in glass jars.

breadcrumbs
fresh usually fresh white bread processed into crumbs.
stale made by blending or processing one- or two-day-old bread.

burghul hulled steamed wheat kernels also known as bulghur wheat. Is not the same as cracked wheat.

cajun seasoning packaged blend of assorted herbs and spices including paprika, basil, onion, fennel, thyme, cayenne and tarragon.

capers the grey-green buds of a warm climate (usually Mediterranean) shrub, sold either dried and salted or pickled in a vinegar brine. *Baby capers* are smaller, fuller-flavoured and more expensive than the full-sized ones. Capers should be rinsed well before using.

capsicum also known as bell pepper or, simply, pepper; they can be red, green, yellow, orange or purplish black. Seeds and membranes should be discarded before use.

cheese
bocconcini a walnut-sized baby mozzarella.
haloumi a cream-coloured, firm, sheep-milk cheese; somewhat like a minty, salty fetta in flavour. Can be grilled or fried, briefly, without breaking down.
parmesan also known as parmigiano; a hard, grainy cow-milk cheese.

chickpeas also called garbanzos, hummus or channa; an irregularly round, sandy-coloured legume.

chilli generally the smaller the chilli, the hotter it is. Use rubber gloves when seeding and chopping fresh chillies to prevent burning your skin.
thai red small, hot and bright red in colour.

ciabatta in Italian, the word means slipper, which is the traditional shape of this popular white bread with a crisp crust.

coriander also known as pak chee, cilantro or chinese parsley; bright-green leafy herb with a pungent flavour. Also available as seeds or ground, but these are no substitute for fresh coriander, as the taste is very different.

cucumber
lebanese short, slender and thin-skinned. The most popular variety because of its tender, edible skin, tiny, yielding seeds and sweet, fresh taste.

telegraph long and green with ridges running down its entire length; also known as continental cucumber.

cumin also known as zeera.

eggplant also known as aubergine. Ranges in size from tiny to very large.

fish
firm white fish fillets from a non-oily fish including bream, flathead, whiting, snapper, jewfish and ling.
swordfish also known as broadbill. Substitute with yellowfin or bluefin tuna or mahi mahi or any firm white fish.

five-spice powder a mixture of ground cinnamon, cloves, star anise, sichuan pepper and fennel seeds. Also known as chinese five-spice.

flour, plain an all-purpose flour made from wheat.

garam masala a blend of spices based on cloves, cardamom, cinnamon, coriander, fennel and cumin, roasted and ground together.

ginger also known as green or root ginger; the thick root of a tropical plant. Powered ginger cannot be substituted for fresh ginger.
green ginger wine has the taste of fresh ginger; has a high alcohol content. Can be substituted with dry (white) vermouth, if you prefer.

lemon grass a tall, clumping, lemon-smelling and -tasting, sharp-edged grass.

lemon pepper seasoning a blend of crushed black pepper, lemon, herbs and spices.

mirin a champagne-coloured cooking wine from Japan; made from glutinous rice and alcohol and used expressly for cooking. Should not be confused with sake.

paprika ground dried sweet red capsicum (bell pepper); available as sweet, hot, mild and smoked.

parsley, flat-leaf also known as continental parsley or italian parsley.

patty-pan squash also known as crookneck or custard marrow pumpkins.

pesto a classic uncooked sauce made from basil, garlic, parmesan and olive oil; often served over pasta. Now also available made from sun-dried tomatoes.

pitta also known as lebanese bread; wheat-flour pocket bread sold in large, flat pieces that separate into two thin rounds. Also available in small thick pieces called pocket pitta.

prawns also known as shrimp.

rocket also known as arugula, rugula and rucola. *Baby rocket leaves* are smaller and less peppery.

sauces
  barbecue a spicy, tomato-based sauce used as an accompaniment or baste.

  fish also called nam pla or nuoc nam; made from pulverised salted fermented fish, most often anchovies. Has a pungent smell and strong taste; use sparingly.

  hoisin a thick, sweet and spicy Chinese paste made from salted fermented soy beans, onions and garlic.

  plum made from plums, vinegar, sugar, chillies and spices.

  soy also known as sieu. *Dark soy* is deep brown, almost black in colour; rich, with a thicker consistency than other types. *Light soy* is a thin, pale, salty-tasting sauce.

  sweet chilli a mild sauce made from red chillies, sugar, garlic and vinegar.

  tomato also known as ketchup or catsup.

  worcestershire a thin, dark-brown spicy sauce.

starfruit also known as carambola, five-corner fruit or chinese star fruit; pale green or yellow colour, it has a clean, crisp texture.

sugar
  palm also known as nam tan pip, jaggery, jawa or gula melaka; made from the sap of the sugar palm tree. Light brown to black in colour and usually sold in rock-hard cakes; the sugar of choice in Indian and most South-East Asian cooking. Substitute it with brown sugar if unavailable.

  raw natural brown granulated sugar.

  white also known as crystal or granulated table sugar.

tahini sesame seed paste available from Middle Eastern food stores.

teriyaki marinade a Japanese sauce made from soy sauce, mirin, sugar, ginger and other spices.

tumeric available fresh or ground. Also known as kamin; a rhizome related to galangal and ginger. Known for the golden colour it imparts; fresh turmeric can be substituted with the more common dried powder.

vegetarian sausages based on soy and gluten products.

vinegar
  balsamic authentic only from the province of Modena, Italy; made from a regional wine of white Trebbiano grapes specially processed then aged in antique wooden casks, which gives it an exquisite pungent flavour.

  red wine based on fermented red wine.

  rice a colourless vinegar made from fermented rice and flavoured with sugar and salt. Also known as seasoned rice vinegar.

zucchini also known as courgette; small green, yellow or white members of the squash family having edible flowers.

conversion chart

MEASURES

One Australian metric measuring cup holds approximately 250ml, one Australian metric tablespoon holds 20ml, one Australian metric teaspoon holds 5ml.

The difference between one country's measuring cups and another's is within a 2- or 3-teaspoon variance, and will not affect your cooking results. North America, New Zealand and the United Kingdom use a 15ml tablespoon. All cup and spoon measurements are level. The most accurate way of measuring dry ingredients is to weigh them. When measuring liquids, use a clear glass or plastic jug with metric markings.

We use large eggs with an average weight of 60g.

DRY MEASURES

METRIC	IMPERIAL
15g	½oz
30g	1oz
60g	2oz
90g	3oz
125g	4oz (¼lb)
155g	5oz
185g	6oz
220g	7oz
250g	8oz (½lb)
280g	9oz
315g	10oz
345g	11oz
375g	12oz (¾lb)
410g	13oz
440g	14oz
470g	15oz
500g	16oz (1lb)
750g	24oz (1½lb)
1kg	32oz (2lb)

LIQUID MEASURES

METRIC	IMPERIAL
30ml	1 fluid oz
60ml	2 fluid oz
100ml	3 fluid oz
125ml	4 fluid oz
150ml	5 fluid oz (¼ pint/1 gill)
190ml	6 fluid oz
250ml	8 fluid oz
300ml	10 fluid oz (½ pint)
500ml	16 fluid oz
600ml	20 fluid oz (1 pint)
1000ml (1 litre)	1¾ pints

LENGTH MEASURES

METRIC	IMPERIAL
3mm	⅛in
6mm	¼in
1cm	½in
2cm	¾in
2.5cm	1in
5cm	2in
6cm	2½in
8cm	3in
10cm	4in
13cm	5in
15cm	6in
18cm	7in
20cm	8in
23cm	9in
25cm	10in
28cm	11in
30cm	12in (1ft)

OVEN TEMPERATURES

These oven temperatures are only a guide for conventional ovens. For fan-forced ovens, check the manufacturer's manual.

	°C (CELSIUS)	°F (FAHRENHEIT)	GAS MARK
Very slow	120	250	½
Slow	150	275 – 300	1 – 2
Moderately slow	160	325	3
Moderate	180	350 – 375	4 – 5
Moderately hot	200	400	6
Hot	220	425 – 450	7 – 8
Very hot	240	475	9

Are you missing some of the world's favourite cookbooks?

The Australian Women's Weekly cookbooks are available from bookshops, cookshops, supermarkets and other stores all over the world. You can also buy direct from the publisher, using the order form below.

MINI SERIES £3.50 190x138MM 64 PAGES

TITLE	QTY	TITLE	QTY	TITLE	QTY
4 Fast Ingredients		Drinks		Pasta	
15-minute Feasts		Easy Pies & Pastries		Potatoes	
50 Fast Chicken Fillets		Finger Food		Roast	
50 Fast Desserts		Fishcakes & Crispybakes		Salads	
50 Fast Prawns (Oct 07)		Gluten-free Cooking		Simple Slices	
After-work Stir-fries		Healthy Everyday Food 4 Kids		Simply Seafood	
Barbecue Chicken		Ice-creams & Sorbets		Skinny Food	
Bites		Indian Cooking		Spanish Favourites	
Bowl Food		Italian Favourites		Stir-fries	
Burgers, Rösti & Fritters		Jams & Jellies		Summer Salads	
Cafe Cakes		Japanese Favourites		Tagines & Couscous	
Cafe Food		Kebabs & Skewers		Tapas, Antipasto & Mezze	
Casseroles		Kids Party Food		Tarts	
Casseroles & Curries		Last-minute Meals		Tex-Mex	
Char-grills & Barbecues		Lebanese Cooking		Thai Favourites	
Cheesecakes, Pavlova & Trifles		Low-Fat Delicious		The Fast Egg	
Chinese Favourites		Malaysian Favourites		Vegetarian	
Christmas Cakes & Puddings		Mince		Vegie Main Meals	
Christmas Favourites (Oct 07)		Mince Favourites		Vietnamese Favourites	
Cocktails		Muffins		Wok	
Crumbles & Bakes		Noodles			
Cupcakes & Cookies		Noodles & Stir-fries			
Curries		Outdoor Eating			
Dips & Dippers		Party Food			
Dried Fruit & Nuts		Pickles and Chutneys		TOTAL COST £	

Photocopy and complete coupon below

Name _____

Address _____

_____ Postcode _____

Country _____ Phone (business hours) _____

Email*(optional) _____
By including your email address, you consent to receipt of any email regarding this magazine, and other emails which inform you of ACP's other publications, products, services and events, and to promote third party goods and services you may be interested in.

I enclose my cheque/money order for £ _____ or please charge £ _____

to my: ☐ Access ☐ Mastercard ☐ Visa ☐ Diners Club

Card number | | | | | | | | | | | | | | | | |

3 digit security code *(found on reverse of card)* _____

Cardholder's
signature _____ Expiry date ____ /____

To order: Mail or fax – photocopy or complete the order form above, and send your credit card details or cheque payable to: Australian Consolidated Press (UK), 10 Scirocco Close, Moulton Park Office Village, Northampton NN3 6AP, phone (+44) (01) 604 642200, fax (+44) (01) 604 642300, e-mail books@acpuk.com or order online at www.acpuk.com.
Non-UK residents: We accept the credit cards listed on the coupon, or cheques, drafts or International Money Orders payable in sterling and drawn on a UK bank. Credit card charges are at the exchange rate current at the time of payment.
All pricing current at time of going to press and subject to change/availability.
Postage and packing UK: Add £1.00 per order plus 75p per book.
Postage and packing overseas: Add £2.00 per order plus £1.50 per book. **Offer ends 31.12.2008**